MURIEL BARNES

21 DAYS OF EFFECTIVE COMMUNICATION

Transform Your Interpersonal Skills and
Build Stronger Relationships
(2024 Guide for Beginners)

Copyright © 2024 by Muriel Barnes

All rights reserved. No part of this publication may be reproduced, stored or transmitted in any form or by any means, electronic, mechanical, photocopying, recording, scanning, or otherwise without written permission from the publisher. It is illegal to copy this book, post it to a website, or distribute it by any other means without permission.

First edition

This book was professionally typeset on Reedsy.
Find out more at reedsy.com

Contents

1	Introduction: Target Audience of This Book	1
2	Day 1: Listen	5
3	Day 2: Count The Number Of Times You Interrupt Other People	9
4	Day 3: Become An Inclusive Communicator	13
5	Day 4: How To Expand Your Vocabulary	17
6	Day 5: Replace "But" with "And," and Embrace "Yet."	20
7	Day 6: Watch Your Pronouns	24
8	Day 7: Offer A Helping Hand	28
9	Day 8: Practice Saying "Thank You"	32
10	Day 9: Stop Trying To Score Points	36
11	Day 10: Ask Questions That Get Results	40
12	Day 11: Refine Your Voice & Speaking Style	44
13	Day 12: Focus On Behavior, Not Character	48
14	Day 13: Uncover Your Communication Background	52
15	Day 14: Understand How Different Generations Communicate	57
16	Day 15: Master The Art Of Communicating Via E-mail	63
17	Day 16: Stop Putting Yourself Down!	68
18	Day 17: Ask Someone For Advice	73
19	Day 18: Shut Down Nosy People	78
20	Day 19: Put Together A Persuasive Message	83
21	Day 20: Improve Your Mediation Skills	87
22	Day 21: Drop The Clichés	93
23	Conclusion	96

1

Introduction: Target Audience of This Book

Ever found yourself struggling to find engaging conversation topics, grappling with how to expand your social circle, or battling social anxiety? You're not alone. There are countless others who share your experiences. In fact, I've faced similar challenges myself. These days, I can confidently engage with almost anyone and navigate social situations with ease. However, achieving this level of comfort was a lengthy and arduous journey.

Undoubtedly, effective communication skills are indispensable for success. Whether aiming to enhance romantic relationships, foster stronger familial ties, bolster friendships, or advance in your career, refining your communication abilities is essential.

Communication should come naturally, yet many of us encounter difficulties. Consider the profound impact communication has had on human progress. Without it, how would we have developed tools, raised families, constructed societies, or established governments? These fundamental skills are crucial for forming connections, exchanging ideas, and enjoying meaningful interactions with loved ones.

Unfortunately, life experiences often hinder our innate abilities. For instance, experiencing bullying at school may lead one to believe they're inherently unpopular, consequently hindering their social relationships.

In my case, being raised in a family of high achievers instilled a fear of criticism in me. Despite being a confident preschooler, by the age of seven, I had begun to withdraw into shyness.

My Personal Journey.

In my early twenties, I came to realize the immense significance of communication skills for anyone striving for a fulfilling and balanced life. Despite having a circle of good friends and dating experiences, I never felt truly connected to anyone. While I could engage in conversations with my buddies and entertain my romantic partners, there was always a sense of something missing.

Observing others effortlessly chatting and laughing at social gatherings, I couldn't help but feel inadequate in comparison. Small talk seemed to flow effortlessly for them, whereas I struggled to find my footing in social interactions.

Upon entering the workforce after college, these same insecurities resurfaced. It wasn't that people disliked me, but I constantly felt a sense of detachment. Being inherently introverted, I frequently doubted myself during conversations and found it challenging to approach individuals I wanted to get to know better.

For a period, I wallowed in self-pity, believing that some individuals are naturally gifted communicators, and attempting to improve social skills without such innate talent was futile. However, with hindsight, I realize how much I had yet to learn. I discovered that communication skills are indeed trainable, irrespective of one's age or background.

My journey towards personal growth led me to delve deeply into human psychology and communication. I became engrossed in self-help literature, academic studies, and seminars, finding inspiration from various authors and communication experts.

While there isn't enough space here to list all my favorite resources, I'm proud to share that I've become an author myself, penning several books on communication skills, social intelligence, and self-improvement.

Through my work, I've had the privilege of assisting numerous individuals in enhancing their relationships and jump starting their careers – a fact substantiated by the positive reviews I've received.

Transitioning from Theory to Practice.

Despite immersing oneself in self-development materials, their value remains untapped until you actively apply the acquired knowledge. Researching, digesting information, and experimenting with new techniques demand considerable time and effort. At the outset of my personal journey, I fervently sought a book containing concise yet impactful communication exercises rooted in solid psychological research. Regrettably, such a resource eluded me.

Now, over a decade later, I've authored the very book I longed for in my youth – the one you currently hold. My goal is to expedite skill development for individuals, sparing them the arduous task of sifting through numerous resources.

Navigating Through This Guide.

This manual comprises 21 communication topics accompanied by actionable exercises, promising a comprehensive enhancement of your current skills. Whether you're naturally reserved, outgoing, or somewhere in between, the principles outlined herein are universally applicable.

I aim not to overwhelm with excessive information but to provide sufficient material for tangible improvements in your social interactions within a condensed time frame. You've likely heard the adage, "It takes 21 days to form a new habit." I drew upon this well-known wisdom when devising the title for this book. However, I must confess – 21 isn't a magical number. Contrary to popular belief, the duration required to establish a new habit ranges from 18 to 254 days.

Despite this variability, the 21-day challenge serves as an optimal starting point for refining communication skills. While you may not entirely adopt new habits within this timeframe, you and those around you will undoubtedly notice significant improvements.

While the book is structured for a 21-day regimen, I acknowledge that life often presents unexpected hurdles. Your schedule may not align perfectly with the prescribed exercises. Fear not – flexibility is built into the design, allowing you to adapt the sequence as needed.

Warning Ahead.

Before delving into the content, I'd like to conclude this introduction with a couple of warnings. Firstly, these challenges are precisely that – challenges. They aren't meant to be easy. In all honesty, they've been meticulously crafted to stretch you beyond your comfort zone. Be prepared to exert significant effort because the outcomes will undoubtedly justify the endeavor. Just like any skill, communication improves with practice.

On a lighter note, I must caution you that enhancing your communication abilities can become quite addictive! As you become more attuned to interpersonal dynamics in everyday interactions, you'll start noticing recurring patterns. It's been over a decade since I began exploring human relationships, yet there's still an abundance of knowledge I aspire to acquire. My hope is that this book ignites a similar curiosity within you.

2

Day 1: Listen

Before diving into crafting your responses, it's imperative to refine your listening abilities. Ever conversed with someone whose physical presence is there, yet mentally, they seem miles away? It can be quite exasperating. Subpar communicators often perceive "listening" as a mere pause before their turn to speak, all the while mentally drafting their reply. This perspective is fundamentally flawed.

Listening encompasses much more – it's about offering others the opportunity to express their thoughts and ideas, fostering emotional closeness, and demonstrating empathy. Today, you'll grasp the fundamentals of effective listening and engage in an exercise to put these principles into action. Listening goes beyond affording someone the chance to articulate their thoughts, though that is indeed valuable. It serves as the initial stride toward personal transformation.

Renowned psychotherapist Carl Rogers, a towering figure in 20th-century psychology, observed that when individuals allow us to voice our experiences and emotions, we begin discerning the optimal route to alter our thoughts and actions. While seeking advice from others can be beneficial, true change often stems from introspection. Having the freedom to openly converse with an empathetic listener stands as one of the most potent methods for this endeavor. If your conversational partner meanders or their thoughts appear disjointed, restrain from interjecting and grant them the space they require. Perhaps they seek counsel from multiple sources before making a decision or need time to process the issue independently. Endeavor to maintain patience, extending to others the understanding you'd desire in return.

Key strategies for becoming an exceptional listener:

1. Employ subtle verbal and non-verbal cues to encourage continued expression: Utilize gestures like nodding and phrases such as "Uh huh" and "I see" to signal openness to further dialogue. Additionally, embrace silence, as it allows individuals the space they need to collect their thoughts and continue sharing.
2. Allow them to speak until they've exhausted their thoughts: Many people yearn for someone who will genuinely listen, especially during times of emotional distress or when navigating challenges. Mastering the art of silence and granting others the opportunity to express themselves fully can be immensely valuable, particularly when dealing with heightened emotions.
3. Refrain from assuming the role of an amateur psychologist: While it's

natural to contemplate the motivations behind someone's behavior, it's essential to avoid speculative analysis, particularly during meaningful conversations. Respect their privacy and refrain from delving into their personal psyche, as unsolicited speculation can be perceived as intrusive or condescending.

4. Avoid interjecting with unrequested advice: Despite having faced similar situations, resist the temptation to offer advice unless explicitly requested. Unsolicited suggestions can be irritating and may diminish the quality of the interaction. Instead, focus on empathetic listening without assuming you fully comprehend their experiences, as individual perceptions and emotions vary greatly even in similar circumstances.

If your discussion partner seeks your perspective, feel free to share it, but observe their reaction. If they seem receptive to your input, continue, but if they show signs of disapproval, such as frowning or crossing their arms, or if they suggest that your advice isn't wanted, pause and inquire if they wish for you to proceed. It's important to recognize that nobody is obligated to follow your suggestions. Set aside your ego. After contributing, it's the other person's responsibility to devise their next steps. Additionally, they might not disclose the full story and will need to consider other facts and factors when formulating a plan.

When paraphrasing someone else's words, avoid simply echoing them back verbatim. While reflecting understanding is important, there's a delicate balance between acknowledging comprehension and repeating word for word. For instance, if your friend expresses feeling lonely and neglected by their family, rather than echoing their exact words, it's better to convey understanding while phrasing it naturally.

It's essential to check your assumptions. We all tend to interpret situations based on our own perspectives and experiences. For example, if you have a close relationship with your parents and regularly speak to your mother, you might react strongly if someone tells you their mother is seriously ill.

However, if your conversation partner has a distant relationship with their parents, they may not expect or desire the same level of sympathy. Avoid projecting your own emotions onto others and allow them to express what the situation means to them personally. Respect everyone's differences and understand that reactions can vary greatly under the same circumstances.

Here's your task for today

Reach out to a friend or family member you haven't connected with in a while and engage in a conversation to practice active listening. You don't have to spend hours on the phone; even a brief 20-minute catch-up will do. Ask them about their recent activities and make a conscious effort to listen attentively. You might be surprised by how often you unknowingly fall into poor listening habits. After the conversation, take some time to reflect on your performance honestly by revisiting this chapter.

This activity offers an additional benefit. By contacting your friend or relative, you not only practice active listening but also strengthen your relationship. Remember how good it felt the last time someone unexpectedly called you just to check in and genuinely cared about how you were doing? You felt valued. The person you call will experience the same sense of appreciation. Perhaps you could even make it a habit to regularly reach out to them.

3

Day 2: Count The Number Of Times You Interrupt Other People

Imagine pinpointing the most aggravating communication habit. While there are numerous contenders, many would concur that being interrupted tops the list. Today, you'll evaluate how frequently you interrupt others and then focus on granting your conversational partners the respect and space they deserve.

Interrupting others can occur quite easily. For instance, during a lively debate, you might feel compelled to interject to assert your viewpoint. Your passion for an idea might overflow, prompting you to chime in eagerly.

However, therein lies the challenge. Even if your ideas are compelling, your interruption may irk your conversation partner to the point where they don't give them the consideration they merit. By interrupting, you imply that your thoughts hold more weight than theirs. As you've likely experienced, interruptions disrupt the flow of conversation and can leave someone feeling disregarded.

Interrupting can convey disrespect. After all, if someone values you and your ideas, they should, at the very least, allow you to finish speaking, shouldn't they? This same principle applies when actively listening to others.

Interrupting can severely impede your efforts to foster a positive relationship with someone. If they sense that you're more interested in imposing your perspective rather than genuinely engaging with them, they may begin to withdraw. This is not an overstatement; interrupting can have a profoundly detrimental impact on interpersonal connections.

Here are effective strategies to break the habit of interrupting:

1. Establish goals and reward yourself: Set achievable targets and offer yourself a small incentive. For instance, commit to interrupting fewer than ten times in a day, and reward yourself with something you enjoy, like buying your favorite magazine or candy bar on your way home.
2. Utilize visual cues: Sometimes the simplest solutions work best. Place a small sticky note on your computer monitor as a reminder not to interrupt others. A drawing of a closed mouth beside an ear serves as a visual cue. Glance at it during phone calls or video conferences to reinforce the importance of letting others speak for building relationships and business success.
3. Prepare your points in advance: While it's challenging to take notes during spontaneous conversations, you can jot down key points before scheduled meetings. Having your thoughts outlined on paper helps you refrain from interrupting. In formal meetings, make notes while others speak, and once they finish, refer to your notes for clarification or to

express your thoughts.
4. Recognize the power of silence: Being overly vocal or constantly interrupting is off-putting. Respect is garnered by allowing others to express themselves and exercising restraint in sharing your own opinions. If you struggle with staying quiet, consider whether your interruption habit stems from insecurity. Some interrupters feel compelled to assert themselves or prove their worth. If this resonates with you, it may be time to explore any underlying feelings of inadequacy, either independently or with the guidance of a therapist.
5. Practice self-restraint: Literally "bite your tongue" when the urge to interrupt arises. This physical sensation serves as a constant reminder to refrain from interjecting.

Cultural Variances

The guidance provided in this chapter assumes that you and those in your social circle have been brought up in a culture where interruptions are perceived as impolite. Generally, in Western cultures, allowing someone to finish speaking before responding is considered good etiquette.

However, it's essential to recognize that cultural perspectives on interruptions vary. In some cultures, interruptions and overlapping conversations are viewed as normal behavior. For example, individuals with Italian heritage may see interruptions as a way to demonstrate interest in a topic. Conversely, those from Japanese backgrounds might consider it acceptable to interrupt for clarification.

When encountering someone who frequently interrupts, consider the possibility of a cultural divide. While it's not appropriate to inquire about someone's cultural background, simply acknowledging these differences can help you maintain composure and patience.

To bridge this gap, you can make a direct request, such as, "I have some important points to share and would appreciate if you could save any questions for the end, so I don't forget anything." This approach helps navigate cultural differences while ensuring effective communication.

Implementing the Practice

Today's activity is straightforward in concept, though not necessarily easy in execution. Begin by tallying how many times you interrupt others in your conversations, then utilize the strategies mentioned earlier to curb this habit. It's advisable to engage in conversations with at least three different individuals. If possible, practice this exercise within a group setting for added effectiveness.

Upon my initial attempt at this exercise, I was disheartened to realize my tendency to prematurely cut off others' sentences. My intent wasn't to be impolite or bothersome, yet my conversational partners likely found it irksome. Even now, unless I consciously monitor myself, I still find instances where I interrupt too frequently. Breaking this habit proves challenging, but your friends and family will appreciate the effort. Who knows, by mastering the skill of restraint, you may uncover valuable insights from listening more attentively.

4

Day 3: Become An Inclusive Communicator

When delving into discussions about politics and social issues, we each hold our unique viewpoints. However, there's a common consensus that regardless of background or personal traits, everyone deserves respect. Today, we'll delve into the significance of inclusive communication.

What exactly is "inclusive communication"? In essence, it entails being mindful not to marginalize or offend entire groups of people based on their individual characteristics. Inclusive communicators avoid making assumptions based on someone's traits and instead recognize and appreciate diversity.

This skill holds increasing importance in the 21st century. With globalization, individuals from diverse backgrounds now collaborate and interact. Inclusive communication fosters positive relationships among people and even enhances business performance. Studies indicate a positive link between organizational profit and factors like gender and ethnic diversity.

Guidelines for inclusive communication:

- Avoid highlighting unnecessary characteristics: For instance, when informing your team about a new project collaborator, like Sam, who happens to be gay, it's not appropriate to mention his sexual orientation if it's unrelated to the task at hand.
- Refrain from assuming a person's gender or sexual orientation: Use gender-neutral terms whenever possible. For example, if your manager is leaving and you're uncertain about their replacement's gender, opt for "they" instead of "he" or "she" until a permanent replacement is chosen. Use terms like "partner" instead of gender-specific labels like "boyfriend" or "wife."
- Discuss disabilities using neutral language: While it's true that many individuals with disabilities face challenges, avoid presumptuous statements like "Peter suffers from epilepsy" or "Mary is afflicted with schizophrenia."
- Focus on the individual, not their disabilities: Avoid categorizing someone solely by their condition or illness. Instead of saying "Pat is a depressive" or "Pat is depressed," it's preferable to say "Pat has depression."
- Avoid perpetuating stereotypes: Making assumptions based on nationality, ethnicity, or other characteristics is disrespectful as it disregards an individual's unique talents and personality. This principle applies even to positive stereotypes. For instance, suggesting that all Chinese people excel in math because "Asians are good at math" is inappropriate.

- Demonstrate respect for race and ethnicity by using proper capitalization in written communication: Terms like "Native American," "Black," and "Torres Strait Islanders" should always be capitalized. When in doubt, consult a dictionary or reputable online resource for guidance.
- Consider the context: Remember that certain words may be acceptable when used by members of a particular group but offensive if used by outsiders. For instance, some individuals within the LGBT+ community may use the term "queer" to refer to themselves. However, this term can be offensive when used by heterosexual individuals, and not all members of the LGBT+ community embrace it. If unsure, it's best to avoid using any loaded terms historically used to insult or demean others.
- Avoid condescending attitudes towards individuals or groups: If you have a disability, you may have encountered individuals describing you as "brave" or "inspiring" for completing everyday tasks like cleaning, working, or exercising. For example, my cousin, who walks with a cane due to a past car accident, has been praised by well-meaning individuals for being an "inspiration." While their intentions may be good, my cousin feels patronized. It's important not to assume that individuals with disabilities seek recognition simply for their existence.

Is inclusive communication truly necessary?

I understand that some individuals perceive inclusive communication as overly politically correct. However, regardless of personal opinions, neglecting inclusive communication can lead to trouble. For instance, using sexist language in the workplace might result in HR issues or brand you as someone out of touch with contemporary etiquette.

Why making offensive jokes is detrimental, even if meant as humor I've encountered individuals who argue that it's acceptable to make offensive jokes or perpetuate stereotypes as long as they don't genuinely hold offensive beliefs. However, consider this: those who do harbor negative stereotypes and possess racist, sexist, or other offensive views feel validated when they hear such "jokes."

This perpetuates racism, sexism, and other forms of prejudice. Avoid jokes that rely on disparaging humor, and make it clear to others that you don't find them amusing.

Putting it into Action

Activity I

During your next conversation involving discussions about different groups of people, reflect on whether you convey assumptions or stereotypes, whether positive or negative. Consider if your language is respectful and inclusive. Take note of areas where you could improve your communication for future interactions.

Activity II

Turn on the TV or browse YouTube for a dialogue-heavy show. Watch for 15-20 minutes and observe if any individuals in the conversation express negative views or beliefs about specific groups. Reflect on whether you encounter similar language in your daily interactions. If so, brainstorm ways you could challenge and address it.

5

Day 4: How To Expand Your Vocabulary

You'll receive more favorable judgments in social settings if you can showcase a diverse vocabulary. People tend to perceive individuals with extensive word knowledge as more educated and intelligent, assuming they can use these words accurately in everyday conversations.

Understanding and appreciating complex language provides a significant advantage, both personally and professionally. Today, we'll explore why having a large vocabulary is beneficial and how to expand your word bank.

The Impact of Vocabulary on Success

Research conducted by linguistics and education expert Johnson O'Conner reveals a correlation between vocabulary and career advancement. Individuals scoring highly on vocabulary tests are more likely to attain high-level positions, even when factors like gender, age, and education level are considered.

This correlation persists beyond merely holding senior positions or interacting with educated individuals. A robust vocabulary serves as the cornerstone of effective communication, which is essential for success. With a broader lexicon, you can articulate nuanced ideas more effectively and comprehend new lines of thought and reasoning.

A diverse vocabulary enables you to adapt your communication style for various audiences, fostering productive relationships that contribute to personal and professional growth. Moreover, it equips you to engage with complex information sources, enhancing your ability to develop advanced skills.

Familiarity with intricate vocabulary also enhances reading comprehension and speed, as you won't need to pause to define words. This, in turn, facilitates smoother information absorption and processing.

Here are some effective techniques to enhance your vocabulary:

1. Incorporate a new word daily: Make it a routine to discover a new word each morning and utilize it during the day. If the word is too obscure to naturally insert into conversation, simply inform someone about your newfound word and its meaning.
2. Utilize apps and online games for vocabulary expansion: Numerous free apps and games are available to aid in learning new words. For instance,

Free Rice offers a straightforward multiple-choice game that challenges your vocabulary skills. Incorrect answers are followed by explanations, and for every correct response, the site's founders donate rice to those in need. Other popular apps include PowerVocab, 7 Little Words, and Words With Friends 2.
3. Cultivate a passion for words: While learning words in isolation is beneficial, understanding a word's structure and roots enhances comprehension of new words encountered in the future. Break down words into their constituent parts, such as prefixes and suffixes, to decipher their meanings.
4. Engage in diverse reading: Expand your reading material beyond your usual preferences to include a variety of topics and denser texts. Dedicate at least 15 minutes daily to reading, as it not only enriches your vocabulary but also cultivates a well-rounded intellect.
5. Don't hesitate to ask about unfamiliar words: Feeling embarrassed about not recognizing a word is common, but it presents an opportunity for learning. If someone attempts to belittle you for not knowing a word, remember that it's their issue, not yours. If unable to inquire immediately, make a note of the word and look it up later.

Implementing the Lessons

Activity I: Your task for today is to acquaint yourself with five new words and integrate them into your verbal or written exchanges.

Activity II: Explore the applications and websites recommended in this section and pledge to engage with one of them for a minimum of five minutes daily over the course of a week.

6

Day 5: Replace "But" with "And," and Embrace "Yet."

At times, even small adjustments can yield significant results. Today, I want to emphasize the impact of words like "but," "and," and "yet." Our choice of words not only influences how others perceive us but also shapes our own self-image. By mastering positive communication techniques, you'll notice a shift in how the world appears to you. You'll begin to see possibilities instead of obstacles, and others will be drawn to your proactive and optimistic demeanor. You don't need to take my word for it—simply apply these principles and witness the change for yourself.

The Power of "But," "And," and Positive Communication How frequently do you encounter "but" statements in conversations? Consider these examples: "I'd love to travel, but I'm afraid of flying." "I want to pursue further education, but I lack free time." "I aspire to run a marathon, but I'm currently out of shape." In each instance, the speaker attaches a specific reason to a problem or circumstance. They imply that their fear of flying prevents them from traveling, their busy schedule hinders further education, or their physical condition impedes marathon running.

What many overlook is that typical "but" statements are needlessly restrictive and negative. This becomes evident when you replace "but" with "and." Take the first example: "I'd love to travel, but I'm afraid of flying." Substitute "but" with "and," and the difference is clear: "I'd love to travel, and I'm afraid of flying." The revised statement suggests that the speaker both desires to travel and experiences a fear of flying. It's a subtle yet significant shift—it implies a desire alongside a challenge to overcome, rather than a desire thwarted by a problem.

When I begin working with clients, I often observe them repeatedly using "but" statements, which become ingrained excuses. These narratives go unquestioned, assumed as truths that dictate their actions. Over time, these beliefs solidify into a script, reinforcing the perception of being unable to change one's life due to an external factor.

Introducing the practice of replacing "buts" with "ands" can lead to rapid transformation. Within moments, a shift in mindset becomes apparent. Hope replaces despair as clients realize that the framing of a situation profoundly influences problem-solving approaches.

Another issue associated with using "but" The word "but" can trigger defensiveness in people. When we hear this word, we often anticipate criticism or negative news. For instance, if you were to express that you understand someone's perspective but suggest an alternative approach, they might feel criticized and threatened. However, if you convey that you comprehend their viewpoint and propose a different strategy, the response is likely to be more positive. This approach communicates that you value their input, even if you opt for a different course of action. It fosters a sense of connection and mutual support.

The impact of "yet" The addition of "yet" at the end of a negative statement can alter its meaning significantly. Consider these examples: "I don't know enough about this topic to pass the exam." "I don't know enough about this topic to pass the exam yet." "I can't get a girlfriend." "I can't get a girlfriend yet." "I just don't earn enough money to buy a house." "I just don't earn enough money to buy a house yet." Including "yet" indicates to yourself and others that you haven't given up. It acknowledges the potential for change, even if the path forward is unclear.

This simple addition shifts perception, presenting you as a more positive and optimistic individual, at least in the eyes of others. This technique isn't limited to conversations; it's also effective in self-talk. It fosters positivity and potential while maintaining a sense of realism. By acknowledging current challenges while expressing openness to future possibilities, it reinforces the notion that you're moving in the right direction.

Implementing the Practice

Today, there are two practical exercises for you to engage in.

- Exercise I:

DAY 5: REPLACE "BUT" WITH "AND," AND EMBRACE "YET."

Every time you notice yourself uttering a negative statement containing the word "but," replace it with "and" instead. You might find that your newfound optimism becomes infectious. This minor adjustment can project confidence and positivity, serving as an inspiration to those around you. If you're unable to apply this technique in conversation, consider incorporating it into your journaling routine. Dedicate five minutes to jot down recent instances of "but" statements. Then, observe the shift in perception when you substitute "and" for "but." Personally, I've found that this simple alteration diminishes feelings of helplessness in the face of challenges.

- Exercise II:

Embark on a "Yet Hunt." Whenever you catch yourself expressing negativity or lamenting a perceived lack of resources, append a "yet" to the end of your statement. You can also silently insert a "yet" at the conclusion of others' remarks to witness how it alters their meaning. While you may feel inclined to encourage others to embrace the use of "yet" more frequently, exercise caution unless you're certain they welcome constructive feedback.

7

Day 6: Watch Your Pronouns

Unless you're delivering a monologue, it's crucial to always consider your conversation partner's needs. Never risk boring them, as disregarding this rule could have consequences. After all, there's no use in expressing your views if nobody is willing to listen. Do you have a penchant for discussing yourself? You're not alone! If you were to ask the average individual whether they enjoy talking about themselves and hearing their own voice, they might deny it.

However, let's be honest – most of us derive pleasure from sharing our experiences. In moderation, this inclination is perfectly acceptable. Since you're living your own life, it's natural to find your own journey intriguing. Moreover, individuals who remain guarded and reveal little about themselves are often perceived as less trustworthy. Effective communicators understand the importance of balancing self-disclosure with respect for others.

Limiting the use of "I" in conversation is advisable.

An intriguing study conducted in 1988 at the University of California uncovered a correlation between narcissism and the frequency of "I" usage during a five-minute monologue. Participants, consisting of 24 men and 24 women, were given the opportunity to speak on a topic of their choice for several minutes. Their speeches were recorded, and researchers analyzed the frequency of first-person pronoun usage. Those who scored higher on narcissism measures tended to use "I" more frequently. However, this doesn't necessarily imply that "I" talk is a definitive indicator of narcissism. Subsequent research has revealed no direct relationship between the two.

Nevertheless, what's crucial to note is that while psychologists may dispute the correlation between "I" usage and narcissism, most individuals outside the field perceive a connection. In essence, although psychologists may argue over the significance of "I" talk in relation to narcissism, the general populace tends to interpret it differently. Therefore, it's advisable to minimize excessive use of "I" in conversation to leave a positive impression.

Instances Where "I" is Appropriate.

Excessive use of "I" may not be endearing, but there are times when it's the most suitable approach. Here's when you should opt for it:

When Asserting Yourself

Assertiveness often requires drawing a clear boundary between yourself and others. In situations where you need to stand up for your rights, using "I" allows you to express precisely how you feel about the situation. For instance, if your partner neglects their share of household chores, instead of pointing out their faults aggressively, it's more effective to use "I" to communicate how their actions impact you emotionally. While others may dispute your interpretation of their actions, they cannot deny your feelings. "I" statements are less confrontational compared to accusations starting with "you." For example, expressing, "I feel undervalued when I return home to find the kitchen uncleared despite your promise," is more constructive than blaming with, "You never do anything, and the house is always a mess!"

When Presenting Controversial Opinions

When discussing sensitive topics like religion or politics, using "I" to express your opinion helps convey that your views are personal and not representative of everyone else's. Prefacing your opinion with "I" also demonstrates an openness to differing perspectives, reducing the likelihood of offense. Countless conflicts could be avoided if people acknowledged that not everyone shares their beliefs and that differences are acceptable.

When Taking Credit for an Idea

While collaboration is often favorable, there are times when claiming sole credit is appropriate, especially in environments valuing individual contributions. For instance, when vying for a promotion in a workplace emphasizing self-reliance, using "I" to highlight your ideas can be advantageous.

Reduce the use of "I" and incorporate "we" instead The term "we" immediately evokes a sense of unity. "We" language underscores shared experiences and similarities, fostering a feeling of closeness. You can seamlessly integrate this shift without altering the essence of your message. Just make subtle adjustments. Consider the examples below to grasp how this technique operates:

"I think the meeting starts at three." "We have to be at the meeting room by three, right?"

"I remember the summer of 2012. It was really hot." "We had a really hot summer in 2012."

"I think that house will be too expensive." "We need to find out whether that house will be too expensive."

Implementing the Concepts.

Task I:

Today's task involves tracking the frequency of your usage of the word "I." Don't fret if you find it challenging to keep an accurate count. The goal isn't to eliminate "I" entirely. Instead, strive to remain conscious of your language choices.

Task II:

Observe a conversation and tally the instances where each participant begins a sentence with "I." Maintain separate counts for each individual over a few minutes. Are the tallies relatively balanced? Do both parties seem content with the dialogue's flow?

This exercise is particularly effective when observing interactions between strangers since preconceived notions about their personalities or topics of discussion are absent. From personal experience, I've often noticed that excessive "I" usage by one participant can lead their conversational partner to appear disengaged. Keep this observation in mind the next time you catch yourself overusing "I."

8

Day 7: Offer A Helping Hand

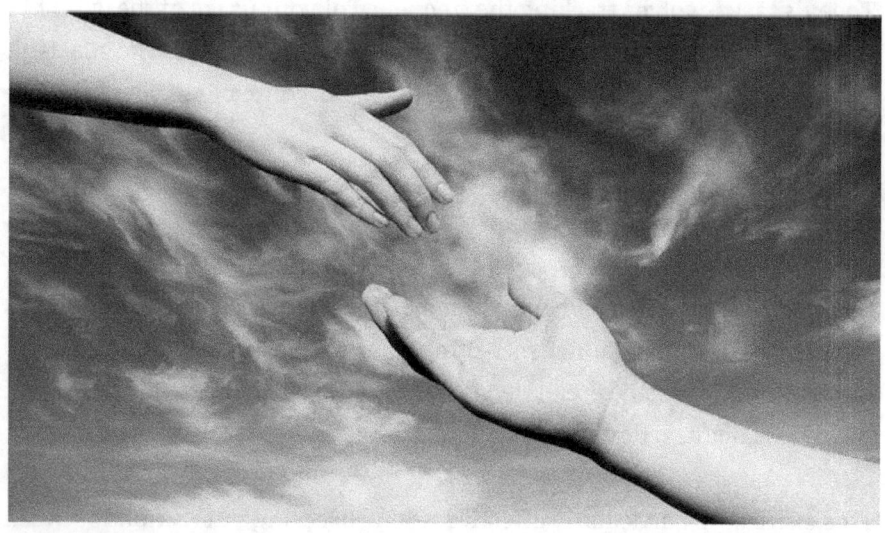

Engaging in Mutual Assistance is Intrinsic to Humanity.

Extending a helping hand to those in need, whether in practical or emotional aspects, fosters a rewarding experience and strengthens relationships. However, offering assistance isn't always straightforward. Today, you'll discover effective ways to support someone in need without inadvertently causing offense.

The Complexity of Offering Help

Navigating between offering genuine assistance and inadvertently conveying a sense of incompetence to the other person requires tact and sensitivity. Without such delicacy, the recipient may perceive the offer as patronizing or intrusive. Conversely, refraining from offering help altogether can portray a sense of detachment.

Here are some guidelines to strike the right balance:

Clarify the Intent Behind Your Offer

When extending assistance, it's essential to articulate your motivations clearly. This ensures that the recipient understands your genuine intention to alleviate their burden without imposing your will upon them.

For instance, imagine your friend has recently moved into a house requiring significant renovations. Upon visiting, you notice their fatigue and the overwhelming state of the house. Sensing their struggle, you wish to offer help without undermining their capabilities.

Consider the following approaches
"Do you need help with this place?" OR "Hey, I've noticed you've been exhausted lately, and tackling this house seems like a massive undertaking. I'd be glad to lend a hand. Would it be helpful if I came over this weekend to assist with the wiring?"

The latter approach demonstrates sensitivity by acknowledging your friend's challenges and offering specific assistance tailored to their needs. It conveys genuine concern and avoids the implication of incapability, thus fostering a more supportive interaction.

Offer Specific Assistance Instead of Generic Offers

Have you ever experienced receiving vague offers of help during challenging times? You share some bad news with someone, and their response is, "Just call me if you need help," or "If I can do anything, let me know."

While these offers come from good intentions, they often sound insincere and unhelpful. It's challenging to discern if they are genuine or merely polite gestures. The takeaway here is to be specific when offering help. Alternatively, ask a question that allows the person to articulate their needs. Consider the practical challenges they might be facing in their situation.

For instance, if your friend's child is hospitalized, you might understand that tasks like grocery shopping and house cleaning can be overwhelming. In such a scenario, you could ask, "Can I help by running errands for you?" or "Would you like assistance with housework?"

Similarly, when encountering minor problems, such as a stressed colleague, avoid vague offers like, "Let me know if you need help." Instead, offer concrete assistance like, "Can I assist you with filing?" or "Would you like me to take notes for the meeting?"

Focus on Changing Circumstances, Not Character

Sometimes, individuals face challenges due to their character flaws. For example, if your friend lost their job due to chronic lateness and daydreaming at work, their behavior may have contributed to their predicament.

However, it's not your role to overhaul their personality or lecture them on life choices. While personal growth is possible, it's a journey that individuals must undertake themselves, possibly with professional support.

Instead, offer practical assistance such as aiding in job search or researching career training options if they seek a change. Attempting to pinpoint their flaws or impose amateur psychoanalysis can strain your relationship and hinder their progress. Offer support or a listening ear, but refrain from attempting to reshape their personality.

Avoid offering emotional support unless you're confident in your ability to be nonjudgmental

Offering assistance by lending an ear or discussing problems can be valuable, but only if you possess the necessary skills. It's crucial to be honest with yourself. When faced with a significant issue from a friend or family member, can you refrain from imposing your opinions and simply listen, even if their choices differ from your own? This becomes especially vital if their decisions might directly impact your life. If you find yourself unable to provide this kind of support, help them connect with someone impartial who can offer a listening ear without emotional attachment to the situation.

Stay adaptable when offering financial assistance

If a friend or family member is facing financial difficulties and you're in a position to help (assuming it's within your means), you might want to extend financial aid. However, many individuals are sensitive about accepting money from loved ones. It's not uncommon for someone to decline such offers. If someone hesitates to accept monetary assistance due to pride or personal principles, consider offering a loan without interest or providing alternative support. This could involve offering childcare during job interviews or leveraging your professional network to help them find opportunities aligned with their skills and interests.

Application Exercise

Do you have a friend or acquaintance who's been facing challenges recently? Reach out to them and extend your assistance. However, ensure that you're aware of your limitations beforehand and avoid committing to more than you can realistically provide.

9

Day 8: Practice Saying "Thank You"

Expressing gratitude is crucial in human interactions. While shared interests and effective communication are vital, relationships also thrive on mutual acts of kindness. For instance, strong friendships often entail an implicit agreement to support each other in times of need.

Today, take a moment to reflect on how frequently you express gratitude to those who offer assistance. Even individuals who have achieved success through their own efforts sometimes rely on the help of others along the way. Nobody appreciates ungrateful behavior or constant complaints from those who have much to be thankful for. Moreover, it's discouraging to offer help to someone who rarely acknowledges it.

Regardless of your status or fame, it's essential never to overlook the importance of expressing gratitude to those who lend a hand. Doing so not only fosters a positive reputation but also cultivates an environment where people enjoy being around you.

Enhance your expressions of gratitude beyond a simple "Thank you."

While a basic acknowledgment is appreciated, adding a few extra words can leave a lasting impact. Instead of a generic "Thank you so much" to a colleague who attends a meeting on your behalf and takes notes, consider phrases like:

- "Thank you for taking the time to make those notes for me."
- "Thank you for standing in for me and gathering that information."
- "Thank you for meticulously jotting down those notes; it was incredibly helpful."

These specific and personalized expressions of gratitude make the other person feel valued, strengthening your relationship and preventing you from taking their efforts for granted. For instance, if your partner regularly prepares dinner, demonstrating genuine appreciation can nurture your relationship over time.

Extend your gratitude by offering to reciprocate their kindness

When someone goes out of their way to assist you, expressing your willingness to help them in return showcases your appreciation. Although most individuals may not accept your offer, they'll still be pleased that you made the gesture. Ask, "How can I return the favor?" or "Is there anything I can do in return?" Additionally, assure them that they can rely on you for assistance in the future if needed. Remember, healthy relationships thrive on mutual support and reciprocity.

Never dismiss a compliment

At times, we may brush off compliments or praise, feeling bashful or undeserving. However, rejecting a compliment is impolite. Instead, respond with a genuine "Thank you," or express gratitude like "I'm so glad you think so." Even if you suspect the compliment is insincere or sarcastic, still acknowledge it with gratitude. By responding graciously, you maintain your dignity and don't allow negativity to affect you, regardless of the intention behind the compliment.

Gratitude and mental health

Expressing gratitude by saying "Thank you" not only acknowledges the kindness of others but also fosters a sense of appreciation for what you have, leading to increased happiness. Studies indicate that engaging in "gratitude listing," which involves writing down things you are thankful for, enhances mood and overall well-being, even for individuals dealing with chronic health conditions. When you actively express gratitude to others, you naturally become more attuned to the positive aspects of your life. This cultivates a growth mindset, enabling you to perceive opportunities rather than obstacles. Notably, research demonstrates that individuals who receive appreciation for their efforts tend to experience better mental health compared to those who feel undervalued.

Implementing It in Your Life.

DAY 8: PRACTICE SAYING "THANK YOU"

Challenge I:

Today's task is to actively seek out opportunities to express gratitude. There are likely several people who deserve your thanks. Take the time to convey how much their assistance means to you. Even for small gestures like holding the door open, offer a genuine "Thank you." And for more significant acts of kindness, ensure the person knows the depth of your appreciation.

Challenge II:

If feasible, go a step further and dedicate time to express your gratitude to a loved one for their ongoing support. Consider reaching out to them specifically to convey how much you value their presence in your life. Reflecting on my own experiences, I realized I had never properly thanked my mother for her unwavering support during my college years, especially during challenging times when I struggled to stay motivated. That evening, I called her to express how crucial her love and assistance had been throughout my academic journey. I acknowledged that although I should have done so years ago, I believed it was better late than never. Her initial surprise turned into tears of joy, illustrating the profound impact of a heartfelt "Thank you."

10

Day 9: Stop Trying To Score Points

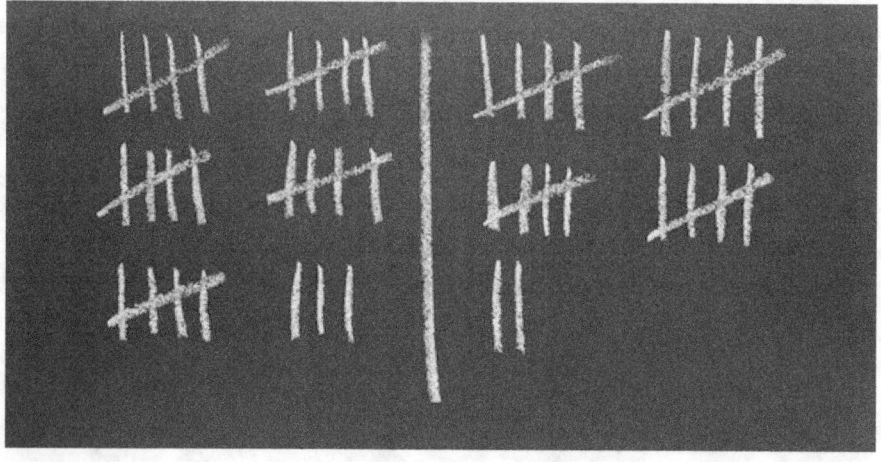

I'll confess, I enjoy being proven right – and I'm not alone in this sentiment! Each of us holds our own perspectives, and it's satisfying when we believe we have the correct one. However, problems arise when we strive to validate our opinions merely to win arguments or force others to admit fault.

Don't be too hard on yourself if you've ever spent hours trying to persuade someone to see things your way. Many of us have been there. It wasn't until my mid-twenties that I abandoned the notion of winning every debate.

DAY 9: STOP TRYING TO SCORE POINTS

In my younger years, I felt like I had failed or appeared weak if I didn't compel my opponent to acknowledge my "rightness." Often, I wasn't even deeply invested in the topic at hand; my primary goal was to showcase my superiority.

Reflecting on those times, I feel embarrassed for my younger self. He was so preoccupied with proving his intelligence that he missed opportunities to cultivate meaningful friendships and romantic relationships. I used to wonder why my dates never progressed further. In hindsight, the answer is clear! Few women tolerate self-righteous men who enjoy telling them why their opinions are wrong.

Needless to say, a confrontational approach doesn't foster positive relationships, whether with friends, romantic partners, or even family. While occasional debates can be stimulating, frequent arguments are draining. As the old saying goes, "Sometimes, it's better to be happy than to be right." That's the essence of this chapter. Let go of trivial arguments and reserve your reasoning skills for matters of significance.

To clarify, I'm not suggesting avoiding situations where you genuinely need to change someone's mind. For instance, if your partner wants to move to the city while you believe staying in the country is better for both of you, presenting your case is essential.

If you aim for likability and openness from others, imposing your views solely to win arguments isn't wise. Engage in constructive dialogue, but be mindful of crossing the line into petty debate.

Consider that striving to score points in an argument seldom yields positive outcomes.

The more aggressively you assert your correctness and their wrongness, the more likely they are to shut down—a phenomenon rooted in neuroscience. In threatening situations, our fight or flight response heightens, diminishing logical thought and reasoning while activating conflict-related brain regions. Consequently, we become less inclined to evaluate evidence and more focused on retaliation. This shift can escalate a rational conversation into shouting matches.

Even if you emerge victorious, it may be short-lived. It's uncertain whether the other party genuinely concedes or merely disengages due to exhaustion. Unresolved conflicts breed resentment, and winning an argument doesn't guarantee it will be forgotten.

Monitor your emotional state; if you feel tense or angry, your words are unlikely to be constructive. If you realize you're fixated on winning without recalling the argument's origin, it's a sign of misplaced priorities.

Consider how liberating it would be to let go of the need for the final word. Embrace the idea that differing views don't demand dissection. If you enjoy spirited debates, seek outlets like philosophy groups rather than letting contentiousness damage relationships.

Implementing it.

Today, the challenge is to accept that others can hold divergent views without needing to correct them. Engaging with someone who disagrees can be difficult, but that's precisely why it's worth doing. Refrain from futile attempts to invalidate their opinions; such endeavors rarely yield fruitful outcomes. Instead of wasting energy on fruitless arguments, consider the impact on your relationships—typically negligible.

If avoiding confrontation means stepping away from a situation, don't hesitate to do so. However, endeavor to remain present and engaged. This exercise will demonstrate that differing perspectives don't shatter the world around you. You'll come to realize that the world accommodates a multitude of opinions, and nobody is obligated to align with yours. Likewise, you aren't obliged to persuade others to adopt your viewpoint.

11

Day 10: Ask Questions That Get Results

When you're in need of quick information, what's your go-to strategy? Asking questions, naturally! It seems straightforward, doesn't it? However, as you're well aware, getting clear answers from others isn't always a breeze.

While you can't compel someone to respond, you can significantly enhance your chances of obtaining useful information by refining your questioning technique.

DAY 10: ASK QUESTIONS THAT GET RESULTS

Here's how to elicit responses effectively:

Ease into probing questions.

No one appreciates being bombarded with a high-pressure query out of the blue. Show empathy for their perspective. For example, suppose you wish to inquire about the likelihood of a raise from your manager next year. Instead of diving straight in and asking about salary increases, begin by asking if it's a convenient time to discuss your role at the company and future prospects.

Choose between open and closed questions wisely.

Common wisdom dictates that open-ended questions, starting with "Why" and "How," are preferable to closed questions answerable with a simple "Yes" or "No." While open-ended queries often yield more detailed responses, this isn't always advantageous. For instance, if you're conversing with someone prone to lengthy tangents, a closed question might be more effective.

Employ a four-part framework when aiding someone in problem-solving.

Questions serve not only to gather information but also to assist individuals facing crises. While empathy and sympathy offer initial support, asking pertinent questions helps devise an action plan addressing the root of the problem. Executive coach Irene Leonard suggests a four-step approach:

- A. Initiate the conversation by posing questions that guide them towards identifying their issue. Starting with inquiries like "What appears to be the problem?" serves as a solid foundation.
- B. Once the root cause of their distress is clarified, prompt them for additional details to gain a comprehensive understanding. Questions such as "Could you elaborate on that?" and "Is there anything else you can share?" prove beneficial in this context.

- C. Encourage them to envision their desired outcome by asking questions that establish what success looks like to them. Inquire about their objectives, priorities, and preferred approach to resolving the issue. For example, determine if they prefer to tackle the problem independently, with a friend, or with the assistance of a third party.
- D. Assist them in formulating their next steps by posing questions that help them outline a plan of action. For instance, inquire if they have concrete ideas about how to proceed and how they will determine when they have achieved their goals.

Refrain from guiding individuals towards a specific response.

When seeking genuine opinions on a matter, it's crucial to frame your inquiries in a neutral manner. This means avoiding leading questions that could sway their answers. Consider the phrasing carefully.

For instance, here are three examples of problematic questions that nudge individuals towards a particular response:

- "Does everyone agree that we should streamline the department?"
- "Don't you think that we should spend Thanksgiving at Peter's house this year?"
- "Shouldn't we put this into action as soon as possible?"

Asking these questions would reveal your own biases. While some might express disagreement, many individuals prefer to avoid conflict. Consequently, leading questions can lead to flawed decision-making both in personal and professional settings, which can have dire consequences.

This becomes even more probable if you possess a strong personality, as few individuals will feel inclined to challenge your assumptions or question your perspective. Let's explore a more effective approach to posing these inquiries:

- Instead of: "Does everyone agree that we should streamline the department?" Try: "What does everyone think we should do with regards to the department's structure?"
- Rather than: "Don't you think that we should spend Thanksgiving at Peter's house this year?" Use: "Where do you think we should spend Thanksgiving this year?"
- Instead of: "Shouldn't we put this into action as soon as possible?" Opt for: "When do you think we should put this plan into action?"
- Avoid compelling people to choose between limited options. This method assumes that you have already considered all available alternatives, potentially overlooking viable options.
- Be prepared for unexpected responses. Never assume you know what someone will say in advance. Offer your undivided attention and have some phrases ready to handle surprising information.

For instance:

- "Thank you for telling me – I need time to process that."
- "This is a surprise, can I have a minute to take that on board?"
- "I'll admit this has shocked me a little, but I'd like to talk about it further."

Further guidance on effective questioning techniques can be found in my book "The Science of Effective Communication: Improve Your Social Skills and Small Talk, Develop Charisma and Learn How to Talk to Anyone."

Apply What You've Learned.

Today, take the opportunity to implement the aforementioned principles when posing inquiries. If there have been lingering questions or uncertainties on your mind, now is the ideal moment to address them. These queries need not be monumental; the goal is to practice acquiring necessary information while fostering a constructive dialogue. Ensure to actively engage your listening skills whenever the other party responds.

12

Day 11: Refine Your Voice & Speaking Style

It's not just the content of your speech that matters, but also how you deliver it. Speaking with an appropriate volume and tone can significantly enhance others' receptiveness to your message. We've all encountered individuals who may not be exceptionally captivating but possess the skill to captivate an audience through their vocal delivery. You too can learn to wield your voice effectively, not limited to actors or singers. Anyone aspiring to make a positive impact should harness the potential of their vocal capabilities.

DAY 11: REFINE YOUR VOICE & SPEAKING STYLE

Today, the focus is on uncovering your unique vocal range and addressing common speaking pitfalls that everyone encounters at some point. Regardless of how compelling your message may be, its impact diminishes if it fails to engage listeners. A flat, unvaried voice can undermine effective communication.

Here's how to infuse more dynamism and clarity into your voice:

Lower your voice pitch.

Studies indicate that individuals who speak in a lower pitch are perceived as more self-assured and capable compared to those with breathier voices, irrespective of gender. People inevitably form judgments based on your speaking voice. Practice maintaining proper posture, taking deep breaths, and gradually exhaling while counting from one to five. Experiment with pitch variations by repeating the same word or sound at different intervals.

Learning proper breathing techniques is crucial, even if you're not actively working on refining your speaking voice. While it may seem obvious, many individuals primarily breathe from their chests rather than utilizing their diaphragms. Engaging in practices like yoga and breath-centered meditation can help relax your muscles and ensure a steady supply of oxygen throughout your body, promoting overall health.

Engage in vocal exercises to refine your voice's smoothness.

If your voice tends to tremble, especially during stressful situations, practicing to maintain smoothness and stability is essential. Take a deep breath and exhale steadily while producing a hissing sound. Repeat this exercise several times. Tongue twisters are also beneficial for honing an even tone. Try repeating challenging phrases like "three free throws" or "strange strategic statistics" until they roll off your tongue effortlessly. Practice these exercises multiple times daily.

Here's another exercise to cultivate a crisper, more polished voice. Move across your vocal range while saying "ney, ney, ney, ney, ney" ten times consecutively. Make this exercise a part of your daily routine.

Eliminate any verbal habits or tics.

For instance, I used to say "um" frequently, which undermined my confidence. A friend pointed it out, and although I felt embarrassed, it made me realize the importance of eradicating such tics to be taken seriously. Besides "um," common verbal tics include "er," "like," "yuh," and "y'know." While acceptable in moderation, overuse can convey uncertainty to listeners. Review any audio or video recordings of yourself to identify and tally the occurrences of these words and phrases. The results may be eye-opening and motivate you to make improvements. If you lack recordings, ask a friend to discreetly capture your speech patterns during casual conversations.

Opt for concise sentences and select shorter words whenever feasible.

Regardless of your audience's educational background, they will find shorter sentences easier to comprehend. While technical terms may be necessary, prioritize shorter words when applicable. Ideally, aim for sentences that can be delivered in a single breath.

Master the skill of utilizing pauses.

Skilled speakers understand that pauses can add emphasis to their message. For instance, a brief pause between two points allows your audience to grasp their significance. Introducing a pause after posing a rhetorical question grants them a moment to reflect on the broader idea you're conveying.

Diversify the pitch and tone of your voice.

Maintaining a relatively low pitch enhances your authoritative tone. However, speaking in a monotone manner will only bore those around you. Allow yourself to convey emotion. For example, it's acceptable to raise your voice in surprise or adopt a softer tone when offering comfort to a friend.

Engage in Practical Application.

Today, I'm presenting you with two tasks to undertake.

Task I:

Allocate at least ten minutes of uninterrupted time for yourself to avoid any misconceptions from those nearby. Select an article or a book and read aloud from it for a minute. Afterwards, record your speech and take the time to listen to it attentively.

Pay close attention to your volume and pitch. Often, we don't actively listen to the sound of our own voices, so playing back the recording might come as a surprise.

Evaluate your voice. Do you speak softly, loudly, or somewhere in between? Is your pitch high, low, or moderate? Through experimentation with your recorder, familiarize yourself with speaking in a consistent, even tone at a relatively lower pitch. Practice the vocal exercises mentioned earlier.

Task II:

The second challenge entails practicing speaking in a different tone during conversations. If you're interacting with someone you already know, avoid altering your tone drastically, as it may prompt inquiries about the sudden change. Human nature often leads us to respond differently to voices with varied pitches and inflections. You might be astonished by the reactions of those around you.

13

Day 12: Focus On Behavior, Not Character

Today's challenge offers not only an opportunity to enhance your communication abilities but also a chance to elevate your social intelligence. You'll discover a straightforward method that can aid in resolving conflicts, fulfilling your needs in relationships, and maintaining positive relationships with others.

Have you ever encountered someone who effortlessly garners respect from everyone while remaining candid and straightforward? These individuals possess the knack for delivering criticism without fostering animosity and swiftly reconciling disagreements.

I once had a boss who embodied this skill. He commanded respect and was known for his candid nature, yet he remained highly regarded. Observing him closely during meetings, I endeavored to decipher his approach. Although he exuded calmness and politeness, I sensed there was more to his success.

One day, I mustered the courage to seek advice from him. As I had recently transitioned into a management role, I was grappling with how to address unacceptable behavior in my team without being perceived as harsh or unkind.

He shared a fundamental principle with me: "Focus on their behavior, not their character." He illustrated this with an example from his experience. Instead of labeling an employee as lazy, he addressed the specific behavior of spending excessive time on social media during work hours. He presented factual evidence, such as the hours spent online and the terms of the employment contract prohibiting personal use of company networks. By focusing on the facts and potential consequences, he facilitated a constructive conversation that led to resolution without damaging relationships.

Reflecting on his advice, I realized its simplicity and effectiveness. By refraining from attacking someone's character and instead concentrating on their actions and potential outcomes, he defused defensiveness and encouraged constructive dialogue.

This approach isn't limited to professional settings; it can be applied whenever addressing someone's behavior. By emphasizing actions and consequences over personality and criticism, it prevents defensive reactions and fosters healthier relationships. Let's examine two examples that underscore the importance of emphasizing actions and consequences rather than personality and threats.

Example 1:

Imagine your teenage son's room is in disarray, and you want him to tidy it up. Instead of scolding him harshly, saying, "Your room is a total mess. I can't believe how lazy you are. You'd better get it straightened up right now, or you'll be in trouble!" You could take a more constructive approach, stating, "Your room is messy and requires cleaning. As this is our home, it's essential to maintain it. I expect you to have it cleaned by the weekend; otherwise, you won't be permitted to use the car on Friday night."

Example 2:

Consider you're a manager, and one of your team members has been consistently late for work. Rather than accusing them of not caring about their job, saying, "You obviously don't care about your job, and you are letting the team down. Start getting here on time!" You could address the issue professionally, stating, "You have been late three times in the past two weeks. Punctuality is crucial for the team's effectiveness. If you are late again, you will receive a written warning."

Moreover, this communication approach isn't limited to significant matters. For instance, if a friend fails to repay you after promising to do so, focus on their actions rather than making personal attacks. Keeping calm and specifying your request, emphasizing why it's important and the expected timeframe, is more effective than resorting to criticism.

Additionally, by addressing behavior rather than character, you signal to the individual that their actions are what matter most. This can motivate them to improve, especially when coupled with genuine praise for their positive contributions. Positive reinforcement is often well-received and can foster better relationships.

Apply It in Real Life.

DAY 12: FOCUS ON BEHAVIOR, NOT CHARACTER

Today, engage in a conversation with someone who has recently caused you distress or inconvenience. This action serves a dual purpose. Firstly, it facilitates resolving any tension and restoring harmony to your relationship. Secondly, it provides an opportunity to hone your ability to address issues by focusing on specific actions rather than making sweeping character assessments or dredging up past grievances simply to inflict pain.

14

Day 13: Uncover Your Communication Background

You possess the ability to shape your communication style. If I didn't believe that everyone has the capacity to enhance their communication skills, I wouldn't have undertaken the task of writing this book. However, it's undeniable that your upbringing has influenced how you interact with others and conduct yourself in relationships. This influence is a fundamental aspect of human nature.

During our formative years, we naturally mimic the communication patterns of our caregivers or primary influencers, as they serve as our initial role models. While some of Sigmund Freud's theories may seem peculiar, he was correct in asserting the significant role our early experiences play in shaping our adult personalities.

I firmly advocate for self-awareness, coupled with proactive steps, as the cornerstone of personal growth. This approach enables you to navigate through obstacles or internal resistance. For instance, you may recognize the importance of expanding your vocabulary or projecting confidence in your speech to enhance your interpersonal connections and social status. However, you might encounter a sense of reluctance or inhibition.

In such instances, it's beneficial to delve deeper and examine your underlying beliefs about your identity and how you perceive communication norms. For example, if you were taught by your parents that displaying confidence could be perceived as arrogance or dominance by others, it's understandable why you might resist adopting more assertive communication patterns.

Jenny's Journey

Allow me to share the story of one of my clients, Jenny, who was in her mid-thirties and a successful lawyer. Her work mentor had informed her that she was on track to becoming a partner at her firm. However, there was a catch: her mentor advised her that she needed to be "more assertive" with the firm's major clients to secure her promotion. Despite reading books and attending seminars on assertiveness, Jenny still struggled to muster the confidence needed to advance her career.

During our initial session, Jenny expressed her frustration, stating that although she understood what was required of her, she found herself freezing up in situations that demanded assertiveness. Intrigued by her predicament, I decided to explore her upbringing through the lens of developmental psychology.

Our conversation unfolded as follows: JENNY: My parents communicated normally, I guess. They were mostly patient, but my father would occasionally lose his temper, and my mother would sulk if things didn't go her way. They had their own friends, and their social skills were decent. ME: Would you describe them as assertive? JENNY: Well, my father was assertive; he didn't hesitate to speak his mind. But my mother... She seemed to have reservations about assertiveness, although she never explicitly said so. Her friends were passive-aggressive types, and she often praised me for being quiet and well-behaved.

As our conversation progressed, it became evident that Jenny's mother modeled a passive-aggressive communication style. Jenny lacked a strong, assertive female role model in her immediate environment, as her aunt, who embodied such traits, lived far away.

Given that Jenny's mother was her primary caregiver, she naturally adopted her communication style. Jenny realized that her discomfort with assertiveness stemmed from her early upbringing, where assertiveness was not encouraged. However, she also understood that she didn't have to replicate her mother's behavior.

I encouraged Jenny to observe and learn from assertive female lawyers within her firm, using them as new role models. Several months later, Jenny successfully secured her promotion, having forged her own assertive communication style in the process.

Reflective Questions

Picture us in a coaching session, where I would pose these thought-provoking questions to you. Take your time to ponder each one as they can shed light on the lessons you've internalized and carried into your adult relationships.

Were my parents adept at social interactions?

If your parents excelled in forging healthy relationships and engaging in meaningful conversations, chances are you've inherited these skills. Conversely, if socializing was a challenge for them, you might feel unsure and reserved in social settings, hindering your ability to connect with others.

Did my parents cultivate friendships?

While everyone's social circle preference varies, total isolation is uncommon. If your parents displayed disinterest in forming connections, you might struggle to grasp social norms and respond appropriately to others' interest in you.

Did my parents impart unspoken communication and relationship guidelines?

As evidenced by Jenny's experience, the communication norms modeled by parents can significantly influence our social interactions. Often, these "rules" are conveyed through actions rather than explicit instruction, shaping our approach to communication and relationships.

Did my parents demonstrate conflict resolution skills?

Conflicts are inevitable in any relationship. Understanding how to empathize with differing viewpoints and reconcile after disagreements is crucial. Without these skills, conflicts may appear daunting and insurmountable.

Did my parents encourage self-expression?

Many clients I've worked with lacked the vocabulary to articulate their feelings, leading to challenges in interpersonal relationships. Often, this stems from parental reactions discouraging emotional expression, even positive emotions like enthusiasm, sending a message that expressing oneself is inappropriate.

Implementation Task

Today, engage in some self-reflection. No need for extensive journaling or exhaustive analysis, but you might uncover valuable insights.

Grab a piece of paper and split it into two columns. Label each column with the names of your two primary caregivers from childhood. While "Mom" and "Dad" are common, it could be any significant figure from your early years, be it a relative or family friend.

Reflect on their communication styles. What lessons did you glean from each of them? Jot down the beliefs they instilled in you. Consider whether these beliefs still serve you well or if it's time to adopt healthier communication practices.

15

Day 14: Understand How Different Generations Communicate

You've likely encountered the familiar saying, "Men are from Mars, women are from Venus," highlighting the perceived differences between genders. While much attention has been given to gender-based communication disparities, less focus has been placed on age-related differences. This chapter delves into the dynamics of intergenerational communication and offers insights into adjusting communication strategies based on the age of your audience.

While the primary emphasis is on workplace communication, the insights provided extend to understanding generational distinctions beyond professional settings. It's essential to acknowledge that individual personalities and communication preferences vary widely. Assuming that individuals will conform to certain behaviors based solely on their birth era is not advisable.

However, some academic researchers suggest that our attitudes toward work and relationships may be influenced, at least in part, by the time period in which we were born.

Understanding and Communicating with Different Generations in the Workplace

Baby Boomers (Born between 1946-1964):

This generation marked a significant societal shift as they entered the workforce, contributing to the diversification of roles previously dominated by white men. Characterized by a proactive mindset, competitiveness, and a strong emphasis on both work and family life, Baby Boomers emerged during a period of profound social change, fostering a skepticism towards authority.

They value managers who lead with empathy and inclusivity, rather than relying solely on hierarchical power. Traditional in their approach, many Baby Boomers are wary of modern work practices like remote work and flexible hours, preferring a more conventional work environment. Dedicated to their careers, they view workplace competition positively and advocate for loyalty to be rewarded.

Communication Strategies: Baby Boomers appreciate detailed explanations of their contributions to the company's success and value recognition, especially for their long-term commitment. Face-to-face communication holds particular significance for this generation, reflecting their upbringing in an era where personal interactions were paramount. While proficient in modern technology, they prioritize in-person discussions for important matters.

They may be less enthusiastic about frequent performance reviews, preferring autonomy in their roles. However, it's essential to convey to Baby Boomers that ongoing feedback benefits everyone and does not imply incompetence.

Generation X (Born between 1965-1980):

Unlike their Baby Boomer predecessors, Generation X individuals exhibit a more entrepreneurial spirit, shaped by their experiences in financially uncertain times with limited economic prospects. They prioritize achieving a balance between work and personal life and value independence over loyalty to a single employer.

Compared to Boomers, Generation Xers approach life and work with a greater degree of skepticism and are less optimistic about overarching societal changes. However, they are more adept at utilizing modern technology and are comfortable with its integration into the workplace.

In terms of leadership, Generation Xers prefer managers who employ a direct and confrontational management style, and they are more inclined to engage in challenging discussions in the workplace. Unlike Boomers, they are not hesitant to switch jobs or careers and prioritize personal freedom, with many harboring aspirations of entrepreneurship.

Communication Strategies:

Generation X individuals appreciate regular feedback and constructive criticism, as it allows them to understand their strengths and weaknesses and plan their career trajectories accordingly. They value continuous learning and creativity, often embracing change and expressing their opinions openly.

While they may not prioritize face-to-face communication as much as previous generations, Gen Xers prefer direct communication styles and appreciate conversations that get straight to the point. They have lower tolerance for lengthy meetings compared to Baby Boomers.

Generation Y (Born between 1981-1997):

Often referred to as "Millennials," this cohort represents the first generation to come of age with widespread access to computers and the internet. They exhibit a greater propensity for multitasking, engaging in various projects simultaneously, and are adaptable to flexible work arrangements when necessary.

Millennials typically view work as a means to personal fulfillment and are more inclined to change jobs and careers frequently in pursuit of their happiness. They readily embrace opportunities to explore different roles within an organization or apply their skills to diverse areas.

Having grown up in a digital era, Generation Y individuals are accustomed to digital communication methods, preferring emails, instant messages, and social media platforms over face-to-face interactions. They appreciate regular feedback and value leaders who encourage their input throughout project cycles, prioritizing a healthy work-life balance.

Communication Strategies:

Millennials consider emails, instant messages, and social media platforms as suitable channels for workplace communication. They expect prompt responses and may become frustrated if kept waiting. Transparency is key when interacting with Millennials; providing timely feedback and adhering to promised timelines fosters positive engagement.

While they respect authority and adhere to workplace regulations, Millennials seek transparency in decision-making processes and rationale behind directives. Clear communication and acknowledgment of their contributions are crucial for effectively engaging with this generation.

Generation Z (Born from 1998 onwards):

This generation has grown up amidst a surge in social justice movements, placing a significant emphasis on inclusive communication. They are deeply passionate about issues such as transgender rights, combating workplace sexism, and addressing social injustices like racism and income inequality.

Raised in a digital era, Gen Z individuals are accustomed to remote work, online collaboration, and engaging with a diverse array of clients and organizations. They are less likely to remain under the same employer for an extended period, valuing flexibility and adaptability in their careers.

With a keen awareness of technology's privacy and security implications, Gen Z embraces social media but recognizes the permanence of online content. Enhanced globalization and access to information have broadened their career horizons, fostering independence, innovation, and a desire for financial stability.

Communication Strategies:

Inclusive communication is paramount when interacting with Gen Z, given their diverse backgrounds. With over 50% of under-18s expected to be from minority ethnic groups or races by 2020, organizations must tailor their communication policies accordingly.

Gen Z individuals are eager learners who appreciate opportunities to voice their opinions. While similar to Millennials in many aspects, they value anonymous communication and are cautious about managing their online presence. For sensitive discussions, they may prefer face-to-face meetings to avoid leaving digital traces.

Implementation:

Take a moment to reflect on your interactions with individuals from different generations in your professional or social circles. Do you find it equally easy to connect with those significantly older or younger than yourself?

Identify someone from another generation with whom you've previously struggled to establish rapport. Considering the insights from this chapter, contemplate whether age disparities may have contributed to the challenges you've encountered.

If you believe age differences could be a factor, your objective today is to attempt to engage with this individual in a fresh manner. Your approach will vary based on the specific circumstances. For instance, suppose you're collaborating on a project involving two Baby Boomers and one Generation X member. While the Boomers prefer weekly progress updates, the Gen Xer appears to desire more frequent guidance.

Recognizing that Gen Xers typically value ongoing feedback, you might opt to touch base with them every few days instead. This adjustment demonstrates respect for their communication preferences and fosters more cohesive working relationships.

16

Day 15: Master The Art Of Communicating Via E-mail

In today's digital age, the widespread use of email and social media has become commonplace, both in professional and personal contexts. These platforms offer convenience, cost-effectiveness, and ample opportunity for self-expression. However, it's essential to exercise caution, as text-based messages can often be misinterpreted, leading to potentially detrimental outcomes, particularly in professional settings where emails represent a company's image.

An alarming statistic reveals that recipients misinterpret the tone and intent of emails up to half the time. What's more concerning is that many individuals believe they can accurately discern the underlying message of a sender. In this section, you'll discover strategies to consistently strike the right tone in your emails.

Outlined below are fundamental guidelines for crafting effective emails that effectively convey your message:

Mirror the Tone of the Recipient:

When corresponding with someone in a senior position, adopt a tone that aligns with theirs. If they employ formal language, follow suit. Conversely, if they adopt a more casual tone, you can adjust accordingly. In the absence of clear cues, default to formal business language.

Facilitate Clarification:

When discussing complex issues or sharing extensive information, provide recipients with alternative means of communication for follow-up. This is especially crucial for time-sensitive matters. Ensure they have access to your phone number in addition to your email address for immediate contact.

Maintain Conciseness with Warmth:

While keeping emails concise, refrain from appearing overly abrupt. Avoid sending terse requests or statements without context, as they can come across as demanding or impersonal. Unlike face-to-face interactions where tone and demeanor convey nuances, written communication lacks these cues, necessitating clarity and warmth through explicit language.

Additionally, consider punctuation's role in conveying tone accurately. Exclamation points should be sparingly used to avoid conveying unintended intensity or aggression. Proper punctuation enhances clarity and fosters positive communication dynamics. Ultimately, adopting a friendly, considerate tone in your emails contributes to stronger professional relationships and effective communication channels.

Keep your email subject line concise:

If you find it challenging to come up with a brief subject line, it's likely that your email contains too much information. Refocus on the primary purpose of your message and consider revising it if necessary. With the average businessperson receiving over 100 emails daily, it's crucial to make it easy for them to identify the key points of your message.

Consider the recipient reading over your shoulder:

Before hitting "Send," review your message as if the recipient were present in the room with you. Ensure that your email does not contain any inappropriate remarks that you wouldn't feel comfortable saying face-to-face. Remember, emails endure over time, and what may seem harmless could be offensive in perpetuity.

Provide context for attachments:

When including attachments, mention them within the body of your email. Use clear and relevant titles for your attachments to reassure the recipient that they are safe to open without any risk.

Utilize email templates:

For those who struggle with writing or lack the time to craft detailed messages, consider using email templates. Numerous free resources offer pre-written templates tailored for various business needs, saving you time and effort. You can also create your own templates based on well-structured emails you've previously composed or adapt templates from others, ensuring to remove any identifying information.

Incorporate a lighthearted disclaimer:

When feeling stressed, fatigued, or frustrated, add a brief humorous disclaimer at the beginning or end of your email to acknowledge your mood but maintain a positive tone.

Close with "Thanks in advance" where appropriate:

Studies have shown that using phrases like "Thanks in advance" can significantly increase response rates in business emails. Considering the importance of email in professional communication, employing effective closing phrases can enhance your email's impact.

Simplify your language:

Unless familiar with the recipient's preferences, aim to write in language accessible to a third-grader. Using straightforward language and concise sentences not only aids comprehension but also minimizes the risk of cross-cultural misunderstandings.

Avoid emojis in formal communication:

Emojis, GIFs, and novelty filters should be reserved for informal exchanges and personal conversations. In professional settings, refrain from using such elements in emails to maintain a professional tone and avoid potential misinterpretations.

Apply It.

DAY 15: MASTER THE ART OF COMMUNICATING VIA E-MAIL

Chances are, you'll need to send an email today. Before hitting "Send," take a moment to read it aloud. This simple practice can reveal if the tone isn't quite what you intended, prompting you to consider a rewrite.

17

Day 16: Stop Putting Yourself Down!

Do you have a tendency to downplay your own accomplishments? Have you ever claimed that you're incapable of doing certain tasks, despite having proven otherwise in the past? Maybe you even engage in self-criticism frequently. Moments of doubt are common for everyone, and it's beneficial to reflect on areas where we can improve.

However, there's a significant distinction between maintaining humility and excessively criticizing yourself in front of others. Today, we'll explore why belittling yourself is a harmful communication pattern that negatively impacts your relationships, well-being, and professional advancement.

Why do we engage in self-deprecation in the first place?

Well, there are several reasons:

Firstly, many of us fear being perceived as arrogant.

Some believe that by criticizing ourselves, we prevent the development of a swollen ego. However, there's a downside to this approach. Constantly highlighting our flaws can actually be self-centered and may make us appear tedious or entitled to others. It's important not to burden those around us with unnecessary negativity that they don't wish to hear; it only wastes their valuable time and could lead to resentment.

Alternatively, we might downplay our achievements to prevent others from feeling jealous or to shield ourselves from bullying. Unfortunately, many bright students are subjected to bullying in school for being labeled as "nerds," leading them to adopt self-deprecation as a defense mechanism. If you were one of those students, you may carry this behavior into adulthood, affecting both your professional life and personal relationships.

Our upbringing may contribute to this behavior:

Consider the communication patterns you observed from your parents or caregivers while growing up. Children often mimic the habits of their parents, so if they frequently belittled themselves, you might have internalized this behavior as normal.

Fear of failure drives us to preemptively devalue ourselves:

By proclaiming our incompetence beforehand, we hope to cushion the blow of potential failure. This way, we evade facing others' disappointment and avoid explaining our shortcomings. It seems logical in a twisted sense, but such self-deprecating talk can become a self-fulfilling prophecy. When repeatedly told we're incapable, we start believing it. Ironically, by constantly labeling ourselves as incompetent and doomed to fail, we sabotage our own chances of success.

Low self-esteem or clinical depression may contribute to self-deprecation:

Persistent negative thoughts about oneself could indicate a need for professional assistance to boost self-worth or overcome depression. Seeking medical advice becomes essential if life feels joyless, or if feelings of worthlessness, hopelessness, or guilt dominate your thoughts.

Now, let's consider the repercussions of self-deprecating behavior:

Amplification of negative feelings:

Repeating self-critical messages reinforces them, potentially worsening your mood. This negative cycle can spiral, leading to self-condemnation for being so pessimistic.

Missed opportunities:

While close friends may understand your self-assessments, new acquaintances and colleagues rely on your self-presentation to form impressions. If you continually undermine yourself, others may believe it to be true, hindering relationship development, particularly in professional contexts. Philosopher Mark D. White suggests that many of us hold onto a fantasy that others will see past our self-deprecation to recognize our true worth. This notion may stem from childhood narratives like Cinderella's, where a prince sees beyond external circumstances to the person's true nature.

Others may perceive you as judgmental:

Just as you might suspect someone who gossips about others will speak ill of you behind your back, continuous self-deprecation can convey a similar message. It suggests a tendency to judge not only oneself but possibly others as well. This behavior can erode trust and make others hesitant to confide in you.

How to overcome self-deprecation:

The encouraging news is that you have the power to consciously break the habit of putting yourself down. In essence, you need to follow two steps:

Step 1: Practice self-monitoring

To intercept self-deprecating comments before they escape your lips. Admittedly, this is a challenging task, especially if you've become accustomed to highlighting your perceived flaws. It requires breaking a lifelong pattern, so be patient with yourself. Simply acknowledge and move past self-deprecating remarks when you catch yourself making them.

Step 2: Shift your mindset!

Reflect on the various reasons behind your tendency to put yourself down, as discussed earlier. Identify which resonates most with you and delve deeper into its roots. You might need to challenge and replace unhelpful beliefs you've internalized. For example, if you believe self-deprecation prevents you from becoming arrogant, remind yourself of counterexamples where individuals maintain humility without resorting to self-criticism. Problem-solving can be empowering in this process. Assess aspects of yourself you'd like to change, create a plan, and take action. For those aspects beyond change, focus on cultivating self-acceptance.

Remember, perfection is unattainable, and expecting flawless success in every aspect of life sets you up for self-loathing and disappointment.

Implementing the Change.

Today, your task is to keep track of how often you engage in self-deprecation or downplay your accomplishments during conversations with others. By the end of the day, you might be surprised by the total count.

But don't fret! I've assisted clients who made self-deprecating comments numerous times daily, yet managed to make positive changes. If they can do it, so can you. Tomorrow, strive to cut that number in half. Then, on the following day, aim to eliminate self-deprecation entirely from your conversations.

18

Day 17: Ask Someone For Advice

We all admire stories of self-made individuals, but even the most successful people often seek guidance from others on their journey to success. Seeking advice from someone who has navigated a similar path can save you significant time by learning from their experiences and avoiding their mistakes.

Moreover, when done correctly, asking for advice can cultivate strong professional and personal relationships. People generally enjoy helping others, especially when they see their advice leading to the success of those they mentor or support.

Consider this: when someone approaches you for guidance, it likely makes you feel valued. A genuine request signals that the person sees you as a valuable source of wisdom and is willing to make themselves vulnerable to benefit from your insights.

Imagine you've identified someone who could offer valuable advice, perhaps someone established in your field or who has recently achieved success in a similar venture. What should you keep in mind when reaching out to them?

Define your objective clearly.

What specific information are you seeking? Before reaching out for advice, take a moment to envision the outcome you desire. Consider what a successful response would entail. If you're unsure, take the time to reflect on your goals and objectives.

Provide context.

Avoid the mistake of immediately asking for advice without any context. Even if the individual is known for their willingness to assist others, it's essential to include a brief reminder of your connection or explain why you've chosen to approach them. Briefly outline why their input would be valuable in addressing your situation.

Entrepreneur Nick Reese, who receives numerous inquiries from business owners, emphasizes the importance of providing context in emails. He notes that those who outline their specific issues are more likely to receive helpful responses, as it enables him to tailor his advice accordingly. While it's crucial to provide relevant information, it's equally important not to overwhelm the recipient. Respect their time by sharing only the necessary details.

Clearly state your objectives.

Simply outlining your problem isn't sufficient if you fail to express what you aim to achieve. For instance, saying "I want to make a lot of money" lacks specificity, whereas stating "My objective is to earn at least $10,000 from my website this year" is more precise.

This requires being transparent about your goals, which may leave you open to criticism. There's a possibility you'll receive feedback you didn't anticipate. For example, if you aspire to leave your job and become a full-time affiliate marketer, setting a goal to work solely on your business within a year and earn $25,000 in the first 12 months, you might be told that such ambitions are unrealistic. Instead, you may need to devote more time to building your site and consider outsourcing tasks or increasing your advertising budget for faster progress, even if you currently lack the necessary resources. While this feedback may be disappointing, it provides a realistic perspective, allowing you to adjust your goals accordingly.

Admittedly, it can be uncomfortable to hear that your goals are deemed unrealistic. However, isn't it preferable to receive honest feedback upfront rather than learning the hard way later on? Set aside your pride and provide your correspondent with the complete picture.

Share your efforts.

The individual you're reaching out to likely achieved success through hard work and initiative. They'll respect you more if you detail what steps you've already taken. Avoid vague statements like "I've tried everything!" Instead, provide specific actions you've taken, such as investing in PPC marketing, updating your website, or creating lead magnets, demonstrating your proactive approach and indicating you're not seeking a quick fix. Additionally, avoid asking for help on something easily searchable online.

Offer a compliment.

Conclude your message with a brief acknowledgment of how their work has benefited you. Regardless of their status, most people appreciate positive feedback. Keep it genuine and concise, such as mentioning admiration for a recent article they've written on a specific topic.

Utilize mutual connections.

If you share acquaintances with the person you're contacting, seek insights from them. Inquire about any sensitive topics to avoid or successful communication strategies used by others who sought advice from the individual. Consider requesting to review previous emails sent to them for guidance on crafting your message.

Adapt your tone and style.

Review the recipient's website or social media presence to gauge their preferred communication style. If they employ formal language and technical terms, adopt a professional tone. Conversely, if they present themselves as approachable and informal, opt for a casual approach. When in doubt, choose a conservative style to err on the side of caution.

Encourage further communication.

If corresponding via email, express your anticipation of potentially meeting in person at an upcoming event or conference. This demonstrates your eagerness to establish a relationship with them.

Always express gratitude, whether through a follow-up email or a polite thank-you note, upon receiving a response. While no one owes you their time, showing appreciation is essential for building and maintaining professional connections.

Implementing the Advice.

Do you find yourself grappling with a persistent problem that's been weighing on your mind? Whether it's a personal or professional issue, significant or minor, your challenge today is to seek guidance from someone else. Keep in mind that while you're open to receiving advice, you're not obligated to follow it if you believe it won't suit your situation. The goal here is to practice formulating a request and summoning the courage to send it out.

19

Day 18: Shut Down Nosy People

Humans naturally possess a sense of curiosity, but some individuals take this curiosity to excessive levels, bordering on nosiness. If you find yourself uncomfortable with someone bombarding you with inappropriate questions, today's exercise could prove invaluable.

Many nosy individuals may not even realize they're being intrusive or that their questions are unwelcome. Fortunately, there are effective ways to tactfully deflect them.

Here are some strategies to employ when faced with someone who just won't take the hint. It's crucial to select the tactics that best align with your situation and the individual's personality.

If you suspect they are bored, give them a task to do.

If you suspect they're seeking entertainment rather than genuinely interested in your personal life, provide them with a task. Some nosy people might simply be trying to alleviate boredom. Instead of indulging their intrusive questions, offer them an alternative activity.

For instance, imagine a coworker who routinely interrupts your workday with idle chatter. Here's a way to address the situation: Coworker: Hi! How are you? You: Oh, swamped. Do you need anything? Coworker: Not really. So, how was your weekend? I went fishing. Caught a ten-pound... You: Great! Do you have a moment? I could really use your help with something. My task list is overwhelming. Would you mind assisting with photocopies or filing?

By consistently redirecting their attention to tasks whenever they drop by "for a chat," they'll soon grasp the message. However, ensure that implementing this technique won't jeopardize your position within the company. From an HR perspective, there may be instances where this approach isn't appropriate. For example, if the nosy coworker holds a higher position than you, it wouldn't be suitable to ask them to handle menial tasks. Always exercise sound judgment in such situations.

Reverse the focus.

While it's not a universal rule, I've observed that nosy individuals often enjoy discussing themselves.

Luckily, this presents an opportunity to employ the "flip it back" method. When faced with a nosy question, provide a vague response and then redirect the conversation back to them. Chances are, they'll eagerly delve into a personal narrative. You can either feign interest or politely conclude the conversation and continue with your day.

If they're hesitant to share personal details, they'll be confronted with the realization that their initial inquiry was intrusive. After all, if they're unwilling to disclose information about themselves, how can they expect others to do so? If they falter, you can smoothly transition by acknowledging the difficulty of the situation and steering the discussion towards a different topic.

Induce boredom.

If subtlety isn't your preferred approach and you're inclined towards a more assertive tactic, consider employing the "bore them rigid" method. When confronted with an intrusive question, respond to it, but in an exceptionally dull manner that omits any interesting details.

For example, imagine returning home after a tiring day at work, looking forward to unwinding with a glass of wine and sorting through your mail. Your nosy neighbor approaches and probes about your recent divorce, prying for scandalous details.

Instead of delving into the juicy gossip about your ex's affair with your best friend, opt for a tedious monologue about the perils of gossip and the impact of social media on interpersonal communication. Deliver this narrative in a monotonous tone, without pause, to prevent them from interjecting with further prying questions. Essentially, you aim to be incredibly uninteresting.

While it may take a few attempts, employing this technique consistently will convey to your nosy neighbor that their intrusive inquiries will yield nothing of interest.

A similar approach is the "broken record technique." Offer a succinct response and then repeat it until they grasp the message and withdraw. Maintain a calm demeanor, delivering the same response with identical tone and expression each time, without showing any signs of irritation.

Respond with, "Why do you ask?"

This simple question can catch nosy individuals off guard. It prompts them to reconsider their inquiry, and their response unveils their true intentions. If they provide a legitimate reason for their question, you can choose to address it accordingly.

However, if they struggle to offer a convincing explanation, it becomes evident to both you and any bystanders that their nosiness is unwarranted and intrusive.

Maintain perspective.

Keep in mind that nosy individuals typically exhibit inquisitive behavior across various interactions, rather than singling you out for special attention. Observe how they interact with other coworkers or friends to gain a broader understanding of their nosiness.

If you share a good rapport with others facing similar situations, consider collaborating to exchange strategies. This collective effort may provide valuable insights into the nosy person's mindset, empowering you to better handle their behavior in the future.

Utilize light-hearted banter or humor

If you have a good relationship with the nosy individual. Just because someone is nosy doesn't mean they lack a sense of humor. Employing gentle teasing or witty remarks, like "You're quite the detective, aren't you?" with a smile, can effectively signal boundaries while maintaining a positive tone.

Take action if nosiness escalates into bullying.

While nosiness is often merely bothersome, there are instances where it takes on a more malicious nature. Any individual who uses intrusive and inappropriate questioning with the intent to make you feel uncomfortable, insecure, or threatened is engaging in bullying behavior and should be addressed seriously.

When confronted, nosy individuals might justify their behavior by claiming a desire to deepen their relationship with you or even offer assistance. In such instances, it's crucial to assert your personal boundaries and communicate that their actions will have consequences.

The most appropriate course of action depends on the seriousness and context of the situation. Sometimes, simply informing someone that failure to respect your privacy will result in the termination of the conversation suffices.

In more severe cases, documenting instances of bullying behavior may be necessary, followed by lodging a formal complaint with your company's HR department. Everyone deserves to navigate their day without enduring unwarranted scrutiny.

Apply It Practically

If you encounter a nosy individual today, employ the strategies outlined in this chapter to politely but firmly discourage their behavior. Should you evade nosiness today, prepare for future encounters. It's common to encounter nosy colleagues, relatives, neighbors, or acquaintances. By preparing in advance, you'll be equipped to respond confidently when the need arises.

20

Day 19: Put Together A Persuasive Message

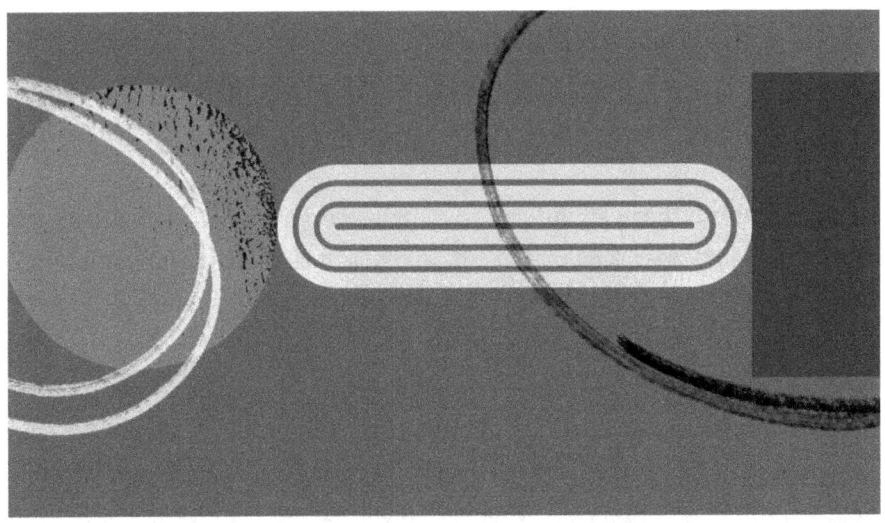

Are you employed in a role where you need to motivate, inspire, and guide others? Or maybe you simply aspire to enhance your persuasive abilities overall, aiming to captivate others with your knack for delivering compelling messages?

Some individuals possess an innate talent for persuasion, but if you weren't naturally gifted in this area, fret not. We can all develop our skills as motivational speakers. Today, you'll have the opportunity to hone your abilities using a valuable tool that will elevate both your speeches and everyday conversations.

Some time back, I stumbled upon a useful technique designed precisely for this purpose. Known as Monroe's Motivated Sequence, it boasts a rich and esteemed history. Originating from the work of Alan H. Monroe at Purdue University during the 1930s, this framework serves as a blueprint to spur any audience into action. While it's essential to adapt it to your specific context, the fundamental template remains consistent.

I'll outline the steps for you, followed by a detailed illustration.

Step 1: Capture their attention. Always commence your argument with a gripping narrative, a startling statistic, or a piece of information that's fresh to your audience. Quotations or rhetorical questions can also be effective.

Step 2: Establish the need. Inform your audience why the current situation is unsatisfactory. Stress the urgency for change and elucidate the repercussions if no action is taken. Highlight how the issue impacts your audience, and if pertinent, incorporate relevant statistics.

Step 3: Propose a solution. Having identified the problem, articulate your proposed remedy. Outline the available options, the guiding principles behind your approach, and precisely what action you expect from your audience. If you deliberated over multiple options before selecting your preferred course of action, elucidate your decision-making process to foster trust.

Step 4: Envision the future. This step comprises two facets. Initially, prompt the audience to envisage the consequences of inaction, employing emotive language while anchoring your points in facts and figures. Subsequently, paint a vivid picture of a brighter future should they heed your advice. Be explicit about the potential improvements in their lives. If utilizing visual aids like slides or handouts, incorporate images or diagrams that resonate emotionally.

Step 5: Outline the next steps. Conclude by directing the audience on their subsequent actions. After all, stoking their enthusiasm would be futile without providing clear guidance.

To exemplify the sequence in practice, let's imagine you've been tasked with spearheading a workplace initiative aimed at boosting productivity. As the manager, a 10% increase in productivity will factor into your performance evaluation. You've been assigned to deliver a presentation to your colleagues, urging them to adopt new techniques as part of this initiative.

Here are the key points you could convey:

Step 1: Capture their attention. "Research consistently demonstrates that a significant number of non-managerial employees lack engagement with their company's goals, leading to underperformance."

Step 2: Establish the necessity. "To cultivate robust commitment from non-managerial staff, corporate leadership must prioritize meaningful incentives for employees at all levels."

Step 3: Describe how the need will be addressed.

Step 4: Envision the future. "Consequently, management has decided to introduce brief weekly face-to-face meetings, lasting no more than ten minutes, to offer immediate and pertinent performance feedback."

It's crucial to note that these meetings may not always entail positive feedback, as meaningful and effective communication necessitates honesty and relevance. Feedback could encompass praise for exemplary work or suggestions for improvement.

Step 5: Outline the subsequent steps. "Starting from the first week of next month, your manager will schedule regular meetings via your electronic calendar. In case of unavailability, arrangements can be made with your manager for rescheduling. Additionally, leadership will undergo continuous training to ensure consistency across all departments. Regular evaluations will be conducted to gauge the program's effectiveness and review productivity data."

For further guidance on enhancing your presentation skills, refer to my book "Communication Skills: A Practical Guide To Enhancing Your Social Intelligence, Presentation, Persuasion, and Public Speaking."

Apply It in Real Life.

Whether your profession involves crafting written content or delivering presentations, you'll find ample opportunities to implement this approach effectively. But what if persuasion isn't a significant part of your job? No worries! With a few tweaks, this sequence can also be applied in personal settings. For instance, imagine you're interested in purchasing a mountain cabin for vacations, but your partner isn't enthusiastic. Begin by capturing their interest with photos of cabins (attention). Then, explain the need for an economical and investment-worthy vacation solution (need), presenting the cabin as such a solution (satisfying the need). Paint a picture of the enjoyable experiences of vacationing in the mountains (visualizing the future). Lastly, propose visiting a cabin together (action).

21

Day 20: Improve Your Mediation Skills

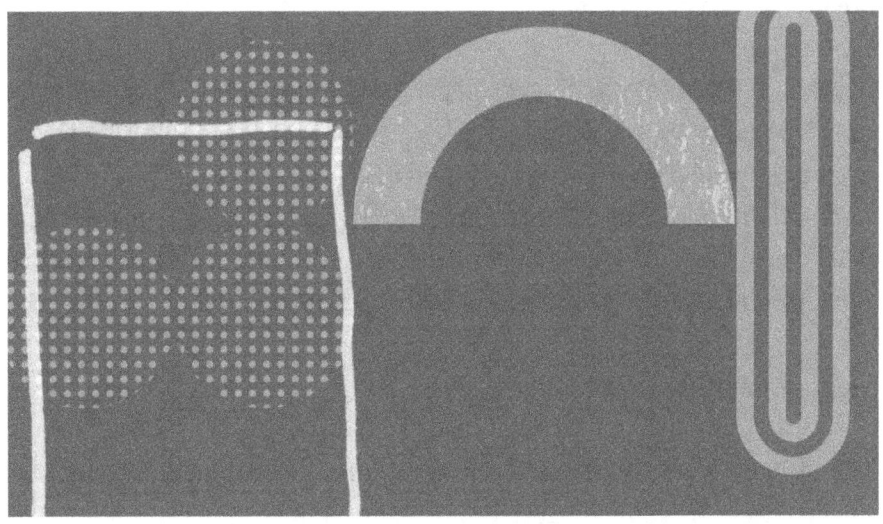

Even individuals who typically avoid confrontation may find themselves caught between two conflicting parties occasionally. So, how should you handle a situation where you're stuck between two feuding colleagues, friends, or family members? In this segment, you'll discover several practical tips to defuse such scenarios while preserving everyone's dignity.

Firstly, let's clarify the role of a mediator. Whether it's a formal position in the workplace or a role you assume within your social circle, a mediator's duty is to serve as an impartial third party facilitating conflict resolution between two or more individuals. The objective is to reach an outcome that accommodates everyone involved to the best extent possible.

Mediation becomes valuable when two parties have attempted to resolve their issues independently but have failed to find a constructive resolution. It's essential not to conflate mediation with negotiation, which involves parties sitting down together to collaboratively reach a solution.

Here's a guide on how to mediate effectively:

Step 1: Assess your suitability.

Mediation should be voluntary for all parties involved, and the mediator must strive to remain as impartial as possible. They should facilitate discussions without imposing their own opinions. Reflect honestly: if you have a vested interest in the outcome or favor one party over another, you're not the right person to mediate. This is why organizations often enlist the help of external consultants for workplace disputes – neutrality is essential.

Step 2: Establish ground rules.

The mediator is responsible for ensuring that discussions proceed in a civilized manner. Here are some suggested guidelines:

- No one should interrupt others.
- Everyone has the opportunity to express their perspective.
- Irrelevant issues shouldn't be brought up.
- Active participation from all parties is expected.
- Focus on one issue at a time.
- No verbal abuse, belittlement, or harassment is tolerated.
- The mediator will document key points, providing copies to all parties

DAY 20: IMPROVE YOUR MEDIATION SKILLS

afterward.
- Confidentiality is maintained unless all parties agree otherwise.

In formal settings, consider printing these rules for everyone to sign, indicating their understanding and willingness to abide by them. Also, outline consequences for violations; for instance, if one party verbally abuses another, a ten-minute recess may be called for cooling off, followed by an apology before resuming. Consistently enforcing these rules is crucial; failure to do so erodes trust in the mediator's ability. If any personalities involved intimidate you, refrain from taking on the role.

Step 3: Develop an agenda.

Clarify to all participants that mediation offers an opportunity for everyone to voice their perspectives, emphasizing the importance of each side having a chance to speak. Individually ask both parties about the key issues they wish to address.

Encourage all parties to distinguish between factual matters and emotions. While someone might feel the need to express hurt caused by the other party, the underlying issue could be summarized as "Party X feels disrespected by Party Y."

This stage requires strong listening skills. Without ensuring that everyone feels respected, the mediation won't yield success. Utilize active listening techniques such as paraphrasing and appropriate prompting. Paraphrasing involves restating or rewording, while appropriate prompting entails asking questions when you sense that one or both parties aren't feeling heard or understood.

Document all raised issues. The subsequent step involves prioritizing these issues for discussion in a logical sequence. While it's impossible to offer a one-size-fits-all approach due to the uniqueness of each situation, the final agenda should be comprehensible to all participants and exhibit a logical progression. For instance, you might collectively decide to address the most recent issue first or opt for a chronological discussion approach.

Step 4: Hear out both sides to grasp the essence of the conflict.

Proceed to address the items outlined on the agenda, allowing each party the opportunity to voice their grievances. Record the key points discussed. If you find yourself losing track of what someone said or need clarification, don't hesitate to ask them to repeat themselves. Individuals fixated on a particular issue or highly emotional may require more time to gather their thoughts.

If one party feels intimidated, suggest separate discussions with each side. Reinforce the ground rules as needed – emphasizing the importance of sticking to facts, expressing problems objectively and calmly. Outbursts of anger or verbal aggression should not be tolerated.

Should physical violence occur, immediately halt the mediation process. There is no justification for physical abuse under any circumstances. Your role is not that of a bouncer or referee. Direct the offending party to leave and involve law enforcement if necessary.

Step 5: Decide what issues need to be resolved

Determine the issues requiring resolution by compiling a comprehensive list of areas where the parties concur and diverge. Ensure thoroughness in detailing these points. Finding common ground can foster a sense of optimism, motivating parties to engage in mediation more constructively.

Often, individuals entering mediation may initially feel disheartened. However, as they calm down and realize shared interests, this realization can break down psychological barriers.

This scenario is commonly observed in child custody disputes. Parents frequently engage in battles over custody arrangements, prompting family lawyers to recommend mediation over litigation.

Trained mediators often prompt parents to acknowledge their shared concern: the well-being of their child. Despite divorce and lingering grievances, most couples prioritize providing the best possible life for their children.

Step 6: Facilitate a brainstorming session.

Your objective now is to assist everyone in breaking down the issues into manageable components and fostering a dynamic conducive to problem-solving rather than conflict.

Remind all participants of their shared goals – primarily, resolving the disagreement – and reassure them that there's ample time to devise solutions. You can prompt collaborative brainstorming or encourage individuals to generate their own lists of solutions. Consolidate their ideas into a single document or display them side by side for evaluation of pros and cons.

It's essential to abstain from expressing personal opinions on the "best" solution. Your role entails ensuring that both parties have the opportunity to present their ideas and encouraging thorough evaluation of each potential solution by everyone involved.

Step 7: Foster consensus on practical objectives from both sides.

This phase may require considerable time, potentially spanning several hours, contingent upon the complexity of the scenario and the individuals involved. Eventually, viable solutions will surface.

The concluding stage of the mediation process entails ensuring that all parties establish realistic goals for subsequent review. Employ the SMART acronym –

Specific, Measurable, Achievable, Relevant, and Timely – to guide this process effectively.

Encourage the parties to draft a written agreement outlining action steps and a timeline, then request their signatures. Should one party decline, it signals the need to reassess the solutions devised in Step 6.

Mediation isn't always successful; it demands a mature approach from all participants to resolve disputes. Understandably, not everyone can maintain a rational demeanor. If mediation efforts falter, try to avoid taking it personally.

Implementing the Method.

If you encounter a conflict today, whether at work or at home, take the opportunity to practice your mediation skills using the outlined steps. Alternatively, if you're not currently facing a conflict, you can still apply the process through the following exercise. Recall a recent instance where you observed a heated argument or dispute. For instance, consider a situation where two coworkers disagreed on the best approach for a project, with neither willing to compromise. Imagine yourself going back in time to act as a mediator. How might you have resolved the scenario? Brainstorm at least two potential solutions that could have been utilized by the conflicting parties.

22

Day 21: Drop The Clichés

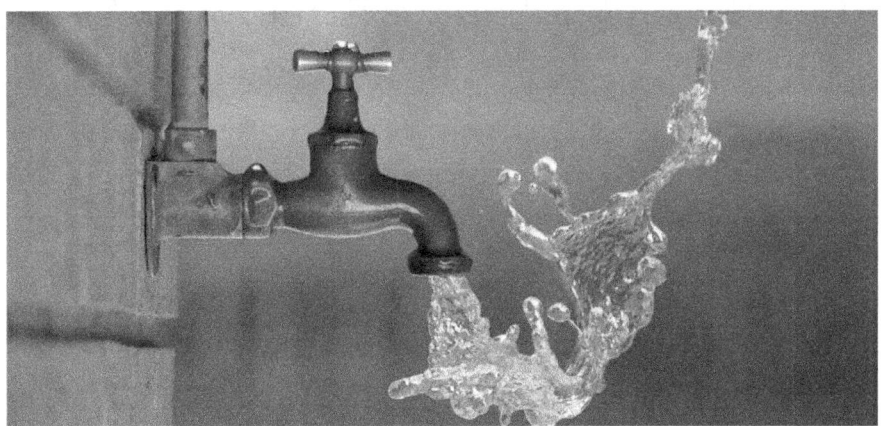

We'll conclude this communication challenge with a straightforward tip that can instantly distinguish you from other speakers: eliminate clichés from your everyday language.

What's the issue with clichés? On the surface, nothing much. Common expressions like "smooth as silk," "Actions speak louder than words," "What doesn't kill you makes you stronger," "It's not rocket science!" "He's not a happy bunny," and "It's a big ask" aren't inherently offensive. Nevertheless, I strongly advise against relying on them.

The problem with clichés lies in their overuse, rendering them ineffective in conveying emphasis. Even if a cliché holds literal truth, it merely serves as conversational filler. While your audience may grasp your intended meaning, your message lacks impact because they've heard those same words countless times before!

What's the solution? Ditch them!

If clichés frequent your speech, you might sense a void. What's the alternative? Here's where you can inject some creativity by devising your own substitutes. Consider this: if you're accustomed to saying, "The grass is always greener on the other side," why not concoct your version? For instance, try, "The apples always seem juicier on the opposite end of the orchard, don't they?"

As you're aware, an extensive vocabulary enhances your image as an articulate and captivating communicator. Discarding clichés compels you to utilize a broader spectrum of words, portraying you as an original thinker. If you can craft your own clever phrases and sayings, even better!

These principles extend to written communication as well. Clichés are easily overlooked. In an era where capturing someone's attention is challenging, avoid losing them by inundating your messages with worn-out metaphors or similes. Instead, eliminate clichés entirely to make room for something more inventive.

If clichés dominate your speech, breaking the habit might require assistance. We all possess verbal quirks, often more noticeable to our loved ones than to ourselves. Summon the courage to ask a trusted individual whether you rely on the same tired words and phrases. As long as you assure them you won't take offense, they're likely to provide a few examples to help you improve.

Apply It.

DAY 21: DROP THE CLICHÉS

Today, you're tasked with two exercises.

Exercise I:

Monitor your speech for clichés and make a conscious effort to intercept them before they slip out. If you find yourself uttering one inadvertently, take note of what alternative phrase you could have used instead. Similarly, remain attentive to clichés in others' speech and writing. However, refrain from pointing them out; they likely won't appreciate the correction.

Exercise II:

Generate three original substitutes for clichés. Begin by crafting your rendition of "What doesn't kill you makes you stronger." For instance, I prefer, "What doesn't knock you down only serves to fortify your resolve." While the essence remains similar to the original phrase, it presents a fresh twist. Utilizing your own adaptations captures your listener's attention effectively.

23

Conclusion

Congratulations! You've successfully completed the 21-day challenge, and your communication abilities are now at their peak.

I trust you've enjoyed the journey and perhaps even unearthed some new insights about yourself. Undoubtedly, others have begun to notice the positive changes in you.

Visit my Amazon page for a comprehensive list of resources, and feel free to explore my website (mindfulnessforsuccess.com) to delve deeper into my background and work.

Regardless of whether you're naturally outgoing, reserved, or somewhere in between, consistent effort yields results. Everyone has the potential to cultivate strong communication skills and reap the associated benefits.

May the fruits of your labor continue to enrich your life for years to come!

"Before you leave, may I ask for a favor? I could really use your assistance! If you found this book helpful, would you mind sharing your experience and writing an honest review on Amazon? It would only take a minute (even just one sentence would suffice), but it would mean a great deal to me and surely

CONCLUSION

generate positive karma.

As I'm not yet an established author and lack support from influential figures or major publishing companies, I value every single review immensely. Each comment from my readers fills me with joy, akin to a child receiving a cherished gift. Your feedback not only encourages me but also helps me reach more individuals seeking fresh ideas and valuable knowledge.

However, if you didn't find the book enjoyable or encountered any issues, please don't hesitate to reach out to me at contact@mindfulnessforsuccess.com. Your input is invaluable in my ongoing efforts to enhance the value and knowledge provided in my books. I'm continuously striving to improve them.

Thank you, and I wish you the best of luck! I believe in you and wish you success on your journey ahead!

Warm regards,

Ian"

www.ingramcontent.com/pod-product-compliance
Lightning Source LLC
LaVergne TN
LVHW020425080526
838202LV00055B/5043